Weight Loss on the Go with Tasty Detox Smoothie Recipes

by

Maria Bertoli

Weight Loss on the Go with Tasty Detox Smoothie Recipes

No book can replace the expertise and medical advice of a trusted physician. Please be certain to consult your doctor before making any decisions that affect your health or extreme changes to your diet, particularly if you suffer from any medical condition or have any symptom that may require treatment.

Losing Weight Has Never Been So Delicious! (Or Easy)

You've heard it all before a million times: breakfast is the most important meal of the day. While it's very nice to enjoy a warm bowl of oatmeal, freshly made healthy pancakes, or a savory egg and veggie breakfast burrito, a lot of the times you just don't have the time to pull out pans and pots, and cook something from scratch in the busy mornings. This is why smoothies have become so popular. They are very easy and fast to prepare, you can add whatever fruits or veggies you have hanging around in your fridge or freezer, and they are a very convenient breakfast-on-the-go.

The thing that's even more important about your breakfast choices is that they can seriously make or break your diet. If you eat something that's super greasy and fattening for breakfast, like a commercial muffin, sugary cereals, or a bagel with cream cheese, your metabolism will have to work hard to break down these food items, and the sugar and simple carbs will immediately spike your blood sugar levels. This will result in the familiar sugar rush for a few hours, and then you'll be left feeling lethargic and hungrier than ever. Of course, it is very important that you eat clean and healthy throughout the day, but for successful weight loss the rule "it's not how you start, it's how you finish" just doesn't apply. How you start the day is what really matters, because in most cases, this will define whether you finish your day on a high or a low weight loss note.

If you're a beginner with smoothies, don't just jump right into the green detox smoothies that are filled with dark leafy and sometimes bitter vegetables. Go slowly and start with some sweet fruit smoothies, to let your taste buds get acquainted to the flavor and texture of your new favorite breakfast option. After a few weeks you can start adding a few veggie smoothie options in your weekly morning routine. Soon, you'll discover which smoothies work best for you, and it is best to stick with them. No one likes all fruits and all veggies, so use only what you really love and what you always have on hand.

In the following pages, you'll find 36 smoothie recipes that will make your weight-loss journey as easy as a breeze. They are divided into two categories, each containing a total of 18 recipes: sweet fruit options for the beginner smoothie drinker and veggie detox recipes for the experienced smoothie lover. Not only are all recipes incredibly tasty, they take less than 5 minutes to prepare in the morning, and travel well in a mason jar, glass bottle, or a covered drinking mug. So, whip up your blender and start losing weight the delicious way!

CONTENTS

Sweet Fruit Smoothies

Tropical Pineapple Smoothie

Prep time: 5 minutes   Calories: 267   Serves: 1

This smoothie is sweet and tart at the same time, and comes packed with Vitamin C and fiber.

Ingredients

1 red grapefruit
1 banana
1 cup pineapple, cubed
1 peach, chopped
a dash of cinnamon
a splash of water (if needed)

Method

1. Juice the red grapefruit straight in your blender cup using a citrus juicer.
2. Add a dash of cinnamon and blend for 5 seconds.
3. Add all your fruits and blend until smooth. If your grapefruit wasn't really juicy and you find your smoothie to be a bit on the thick side, add a splash of water and blend for 10 more seconds.
4. Transfer to a cup or a portable jar and enjoy!

Tip: The smoothie should be sweet enough from the banana and the peaches, but you can add a teaspoon of honey if you feel the tartness of the grapefruit and pineapple is overpowering.

Nutritional Information

Calories: 267
Fat Total: 0.6g
Carbohydrates: 68.4g
Protein: 3.8g
Dietary Fiber: 8.8g

Peanut Butter and Chocolate Protein Smoothie

Prep time: 5 minutes   Calories: 278   Serves: 2

This smoothie really does taste like chocolate and peanut butter cookies, but it is still very healthy and packed with protein, making it the perfect start for a busy day.

Ingredients

1 cup water
1 banana
1 cup cottage cheese
2 tablespoons natural peanut butter
1 teaspoon cocoa powder
1 teaspoon honey
1 cup ice

Method

1. Blend the water, ice, and cottage cheese on high speed until smooth.
2. Add the banana, peanut butter, cocoa powder, and honey.
3. Blend on high until thick and creamy.
4. Transfer to a cup or a portable jar and enjoy!

Tip: Carefully read the ingredient label when buying peanut butter. The only ingredients listed should be peanuts and possibly salt. Stay away from the commercial "creamy" varieties that come packed with sugar and palm oil.

Nutritional Information (per serving)

Calories: 278
Fat Total: 10.3g
Carbohydrates: 26.8g
Protein: 21.3g
Dietary Fiber: 3g

Blueberry Coconut Smoothie

Prep time: 5 minutes   Calories: 238   Serves: 2

Coconut water provides electrolytes that balance the pH levels in your blood, the blueberries are full of antioxidants, and the coconut flakes round up this smoothie with some healthy fats.

Ingredients

1 cup coconut water
2 bananas
1 cup blueberries
2 tablespoons coconut flakes
1 tablespoon ground flax seed
2 teaspoons honey

Method

1. Blend the coconut water, coconut flakes, honey, and ground flax on high speed for 30 seconds.
2. Peel the banana and place it in the blender along with the blueberries.
3. Blend for 30 seconds on high speed, or until thick and creamy.
4. Transfer to a cup or a portable jar and enjoy!

Tip: If you're using fresh blueberries, you can add a cup of ice to your smoothie for a thicker consistency.

Nutritional Information (per serving)

Calories: 238
Fat Total: 4.6g
Carbohydrates: 49.6g
Protein: 4.1g
Dietary Fiber: 8.9g

Raspberry Orange Smoothie

Prep time: 5 minutes   Calories: 250   Serves: 2

Tart raspberries, acidic orange juice, and sweet apples: this smoothie is the perfect blend of all amazing flavors for an exciting breakfast on the go.

Ingredients

1 cup fresh orange juice
1 cup water
1 cup frozen raspberries
1 Honey crisp apple
a dash of cinnamon

Method

1. Blend the orange juice with the water and the cinnamon for 30 seconds on high speed, or until frothy.
2. Chop the apple and transfer to the blender along with the frozen raspberries.
3. Blend for a minute on high speed, or until well combined.
4. Transfer to a cup or a portable jar and enjoy!

Tip: The cinnamon provides with some underlining spice and brings out the sweetness from the fruits, but if you like your smoothie to be even sweeter, add a bit of honey.

Nutritional Information (per serving)

Calories: 250
Fat Total: 0.5g
Carbohydrates: 62.7g
Protein: 2.2g
Dietary Fiber: 8.3g

Mango Lassi

Prep time: 5   Calories: 327   Serves: 1

This smoothie takes so few ingredients to make, yet it is so delicious you'll want to enjoy it every day of the week. The Greek yogurt provides so much protein turning the smoothie into a protein shake.

Ingredients

1 ripe mango
1 cup nonfat Greek yogurt
1 cup ice
2 teaspoons honey
a splash of water

Method

1. Peel and chop the mango into large chunks.
2. Blend the Greek yogurt with the honey, ice, and a splash of water until well incorporated.
3. Add the mango in the end and blend for one minute on the highest setting available until it gets to a rich and creamy consistency.
4. Transfer to a cup or a portable jar and enjoy!

Tip: You can add a scoop of protein powder for an added breakfast protein kick.

Nutritional Information

Calories: 327
Fat Total: 0.6g
Carbohydrates: 69.7g
Protein: 15.1g
Dietary Fiber: 4.8g

Fall Pumpkin Smoothie

Prep time: 5 minutes   Calories: 378   Serves: 2

Pumpkin puree, maple syrup, ginger, cinnamon, nutmeg... All fall flavors into one cup. Simply amazing!

Ingredients

1 cup unsweetened almond milk
½ cup pumpkin puree
1 Gala apple
½ teaspoon pumpkin pie spice
2 tablespoons grated ginger
1 tablespoon real maple syrup

Method

1. Blend the almond milk, ginger, maple syrup, and pumpkin pie spice for 30 seconds on high speed.
2. Peel and chop the apple and transfer to the blender along with the pumpkin puree.
3. Blend for a minute on high speed until well combined.
4. Transfer to a cup or a portable jar and enjoy!

Tip: You can make your own pumpkin pie spice by mixing equal amounts of cinnamon, allspice, ground cloves, and ground nutmeg.

Nutritional Information (per serving)

Calories: 378
Fat Total: 27.4g
Carbohydrates: 30.4g
Protein: 4g
Dietary Fiber: 6.2g

Classic Strawberry and Banana Smoothie

Prep time: 5 minutes   Calories: 216   Serves: 2

Probably everybody's favorite childhood drink was a creamy strawberry and banana milkshake. Here's the grown-up version of that childhood memory that's on the healthier side.

Ingredients

1 cup skim milk
2 ripe bananas
2 cups strawberries
1 teaspoon coconut oil, melted
1 cup ice
a dash of cinnamon

Method

1. Blend the milk with the ice, melted coconut oil, and cinnamon for 20 seconds on high speed.
2. Add the bananas and the strawberries and blend until thick and creamy.
3. Transfer to a cup or a portable jar and enjoy!

Tip: The ice will provide the same thickness and creaminess as the scoop of ice-cream that is usually used in a traditional milkshake. If your bananas are not very ripe, add a teaspoon of honey to sweeten up your smoothie.

Nutritional Information (per serving)

Calories: 216
Fat Total: 2.7g
Carbohydrates: 44g
Protein: 6.1g
Dietary Fiber: 14.6g

Pear and Hazelnut Smoothie

Prep time: 5 minutes   Calories: 265   Serves: 2

The pears provide a nice amount of filling fiber, the Greek yogurt gives a protein boost, and the hazelnuts are packed with heart-healthy fats.

Ingredients

2 pears
½ cup plain Greek yogurt
2 tablespoons hazelnut butter
1 banana
1 teaspoon honey
1 cup water
1 cup ice
a dash of cinnamon

Method

1. Blend the water, ice, Greek yogurt, honey, hazelnut butter, and cinnamon for 30 seconds on high speed.
2. Chop the pears into large chunks and add them to the blender along with the peeled banana.
3. Blend for another 30 seconds on high until well combined.
4. Transfer to a cup or a portable jar and enjoy!

Tip: Almond or cashew butter would also work with this smoothie.

Nutritional Information (per serving)

Calories: 265
Fat Total: 4.2g
Carbohydrates: 51.5g
Protein: 9.8g
Dietary Fiber: 8.7g

Mixed Berry Smoothie

Prep time: 5 minutes   Calories: 272   Serves: 2

This smoothie tastes just like a sweet berry milkshake, but it is completely guilt-free and very good for you.

Ingredients

1 cup skim milk
1 cup frozen raspberries
1 cup frozen blueberries
1 cup frozen strawberries
1 tablespoon honey
a dash of cinnamon

Method

1. Blend the milk, honey, and cinnamon for 10 seconds on high speed.
2. Add the mixed berries and blend for a full minute on the highest setting possible.
3. Transfer to a cup or a portable jar and enjoy!

Tip: Blending the berries for a full minute on very high speed will break down some of their seeds and make the smoothie a lot creamier. The seeds are where all the antioxidants are, so you want to make sure you drink them up as well.

Nutritional Information (per serving)

Calories: 272
Fat Total: 0.5g
Carbohydrates: 64.4g
Protein: 5.5g
Dietary Fiber: 8.8g

Apple Pie Smoothie

Prep time: 5 minutes   Calories: 241   Serves: 2

Apple pie like grandma makes it is probably everybody's favorite childhood dessert. The oats represent the pie crust in this smoothie, the Granny Smith is nice and tart, and the honey provides the necessary sweetness.

Ingredients

½ cup oats
1 cup skim milk
2 Granny Smith apples
2 teaspoons honey
1 teaspoon cinnamon

Method

1. Peel and chop the apples.
2. Blend the oats, milk, cinnamon, and honey for 30 seconds on high speed.
3. Add the apples to the blender and blend for another 30 seconds, or until smooth and creamy.
4. Transfer to a cup or a portable jar and enjoy!

Tip: You can add a dollop of Greek yogurt to replace the whipped cream from the original apple pie dessert.

Nutritional Information (per serving)

Calories: 241
Fat Total: 1.3g
Carbohydrates: 51.7g
Protein: 6.8g
Dietary Fiber: 7.1g

Pear and Almond Protein Smoothie

Prep time: 5 minutes   Calories: 273   Serves: 2

Protein is very important because it keeps you feeling fuller for a longer time. This smoothie comes packed with protein and a generous amount of fiber from the pears and the banana.

Ingredients

2 pears
1 banana
½ cup cottage cheese
1 cup unsweetened almond milk
2 tablespoons flax seed
1 cup ice

Method

1. Blend the almond milk, cottage cheese, flax seed, and ice for 30 seconds on high speed.
2. Core and chop the pears, peel the banana, and add them both to the blender.
3. Blend for about a minute on high speed, or until thick and creamy.
4. Transfer to a cup or a portable jar and enjoy!

Tip: Apples would work equally as good with this smoothie. You can add a dash of cinnamon to bring out the sweetness from the pears.

Nutritional Information (per serving)

Calories: 273
Fat Total: 4.6g
Carbohydrates: 48.3g
Protein: 11.6g
Dietary Fiber: 11.4g

Watermelon and Cantaloupe Slushy

Prep time: 5 minutes   Calories: 134   Serves: 2

Watermelon slushy is a great cooling summer drink, but a lot of times it can be loaded with sugar. For this smoothie we'll use a combination of watermelon and cantaloupe sweetened with honey.

Ingredients

2 cups cubed watermelon
2 cups cubed cantaloupe
2 cups ice
2 teaspoons honey

Method

1. Add all ingredients in a blender and blend until you reach a slushie texture.
2. Transfer to a cup or a portable jar and enjoy!

Tip: Honeydew melon will also work well with this smoothie slush.

Nutritional Information (per serving)

Calories: 134
Fat Total: 0g
Carbohydrates: 33.2g
Protein: 2.5g
Dietary Fiber: 18.5g

Banana and Dry Cranberry Smoothie

Prep time: 5 minutes   Calories: 245   Serves: 2

Cranberries are great for people with diabetes, high blood pressure, and eye problems, but they are also known for making people calmer and happier. So drink up and start singing "don't worry, be happy."

Ingredients

2 bananas
2 apples
4 tablespoons dry cranberries
1 cup ice
½ cup water

Method

1. Peel the bananas and the apples, and cut them into large chunks.
2. Blend the water, ice, and cranberries for 30 seconds on high speed.
3. Add the banana and apple chunks and blend for another minute on high speed.
4. Transfer to a cup or a portable jar and enjoy!

Tip: Use less water if you want your smoothie to be very thick, or add another ½ cup for a juice-like-smoothie.

Nutritional Information (per serving)

Calories: 245
Fat Total: 0.6g
Carbohydrates: 61.6g
Protein: 1.6g
Dietary Fiber: 9.1g

Pomegranate Berry Smoothie

Prep time: 5 minutes   Calories: 181   Serves: 2

This smoothie is both sweet and tart at the same time from the pomegranate and the berries, but more importantly, it's loaded with antioxidants promoting clear skin and weight loss.

Ingredients

1 cup unsweetened pomegranate juice
1 cup raspberries
1 cup blueberries
1 cup ice
1 tablespoon honey
a dash of cinnamon

Method

1. Blend the pomegranate juice with the ice, honey, and cinnamon for 30 seconds on high speed, or until the ice is completely broken down.
2. Add the berries and blend for another 30 seconds on high speed until well combined.
3. Transfer to a cup or a portable jar and enjoy!

Tip: Any type of berries will work with this smoothie, so just use what you already have on hand.

Nutritional Information (per serving)

Calories: 181
Fat Total: 0.7g
Carbohydrates: 45.6g
Protein: 1.3g
Dietary Fiber: 5.8g

Cranberry Yogurt Smoothie

Prep time: 5 minutes   Calories: 212   Serves: 2

Not only do cranberries help with urinary tract infections, offer relief from kidney and bladder problems, and fight various types of cancer, but they also taste amazing. This amazing fruit should be a staple in your diet.

Ingredients

2 cups cranberry juice
1 banana
1 cup plain Greek yogurt
½ cup cranberries
a dash of cinnamon
1 cup ice

Method

1. Place the cranberry juice, Greek yogurt, ice, and cinnamon in a blender and blend for 30 seconds on high speed.
2. Peel the banana and add it to your blender along with the fresh cranberries.
3. Blend for another 30 seconds until well combined.
4. Transfer to a cup or a portable jar and enjoy!

Tip: If your banana is not very ripe, add a few teaspoons of honey to sweeten up your smoothie.

Nutritional Information (per serving)

Calories: 212
Fat Total: 4.8g
Carbohydrates: 34.9g
Protein: 7.1g
Dietary Fiber: 11.2g

Black Forrest Smoothie

Prep time: 5 minutes   Calories: 255   Serves: 2

Black forest cake is a rich and decadent chocolaty treat with sweet whipped cream and sour cherries. We're using black forest cake as an inspiration for this smoothie recipe. It is so creamy and luscious; you'll feel like you're having dessert for breakfast!

Ingredients

1 cup skim milk
1 cup vanilla Greek yogurt
1 small banana
1 cup sour cherries, pitted
1 teaspoon cocoa powder
1 tablespoon honey
1 cup ice

Method

1. Blend the milk, yogurt, honey, cocoa powder, and ice for 30 seconds on high speed.
2. Add the banana and the cherries and blend for up to a minute on high speed. The smoothie should be thick and velvety.
3. Transfer to a cup or a portable jar and enjoy!

Tip: You can use frozen sour cherries if you can't find fresh ones.

Nutritional Information (per serving)

Calories: 255
Fat Total: 0.2g
Carbohydrates: 52g
Protein: 11.4g
Dietary Fiber: 2.2g

Passion Fruit Delight Smoothie

Prep time: 5 minutes   Calories: 191   Serves: 2

Always combine passion fruit with other sweet tropical fruits in a smoothie, like bananas, mangoes, or peaches, because it is too sour to shine on its own.

Ingredients

2 passion fruits
1 ripe mango, cubed
1 cup fresh orange juice
1 small banana
1 cup ice

Method

1. Blend the orange juice with the ice for 30 seconds on high speed.
2. Add the mango and the banana and blend for another 10-20 seconds, or until well combined.
3. Pour the smoothie into two tall glasses or jars, and scoop the passion fruit flesh right into the glass.
4. Mix with a straw and enjoy.

Tip: Any sweet tropical fruit will work with this smoothie.

Nutritional Information (per serving)

Calories: 191
Fat Total: 0.7g
Carbohydrates: 46.2g
Protein: 2.3g
Dietary Fiber: 5.5g

Kiwi Antioxidant Smoothie

Prep time: 5 minutes   Calories: 244   Serves: 2

Kiwifruit is loaded with Vitamin C, Vitamin E, and Vitamin A, which are three of the most important antioxidants.

Ingredients

4 kiwis
1 large pineapple
½ cup fresh orange juice
½ cup water
1 cup ice
a dash of cinnamon

Method

1. Blend the orange juice, water, ice, and cinnamon for 30 seconds on high speed.
2. Peel and cube the pineapple and the kiwi fruit.
3. Add them to your blender and blend for another 30 seconds on the highest setting possible.
4. Transfer to a cup or a portable jar and enjoy!

Tip: If you don't have a high speed blender, blend for a minute longer to break down all the kiwi seeds. They can make your smoothie taste somewhat bitter.

Nutritional Information (per serving)

Calories: 244
Fat Total: 1.2g
Carbohydrates: 61.3g
Protein: 3.5g
Dietary Fiber: 8.2g

Veggie Detox Smoothies

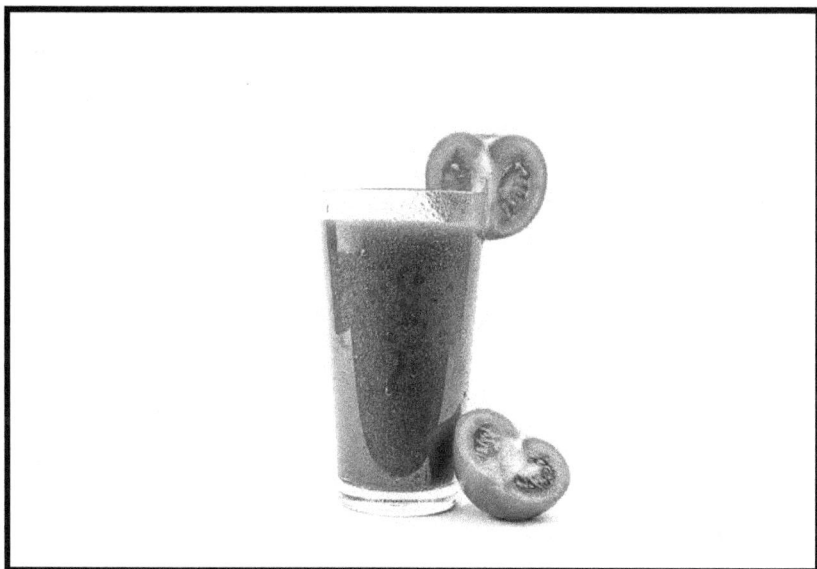

A lot of people think that embarking on a detox journey means constantly chomping down kale and bitter grapefruit juice, and they are terribly wrong. When you detox, your body will slowly eliminate all toxins that have bulked up from junk food, pesticides, and chemicals; and will start replenishing and regenerating its cells. This process <u>will</u> happen as long as you eat tons of fruits and veggies, preferable by juicing or blending. Yes, all fruits and veggies have detox benefits: they are filled with various nutrients, vitamins, and minerals which aide your body to cleanse itself from the inside. However, veggies are a much greater asset in detox, especially the green ones, because even though fruits are very healthy, they still contain a lot of carbs and sugars. These can be troubling for your digestive tracts, especially when you're trying to detox.

These veggie filled smoothie recipes will help your body heal itself through detox.

Glowing Skin Smoothie

Prep time: 5 minutes   Calories: 212   Serves: 1

This smoothie is just loaded with antioxidants and flavonoids. Drink it once a day for three weeks and your skin will shine like it never has before.

Ingredients

1 cup kale
½ head romaine lettuce
1 celery stalk
½ banana
1 green apple
juice from one lemon
1 cup water

Method

1. Blend the lemon juice and water for 10 seconds, or until foamy.
2. Add all the vegetables and blend for another 20 seconds, or until they are all broken up.
3. Add the banana and the apple. Blend for another 30 seconds, or until well incorporated.
4. Transfer to a cup or a portable jar and enjoy!

Tip: You can sub the kale for some spinach, and use a pear instead of the apple.

Nutritional Information

Calories: 212
Fat Total: 0.4g
Carbohydrates: 56.3g
Protein: 4.8g
Dietary Fiber: 11g

Biotin Chard Smoothie

Prep time: 5 minutes   Calories: 287   Serves: 2

Biotin is great for beautiful hair and nails, and this smoothie combines all of the most potent fruit and veggie sources of the vitamin.

Ingredients

4 giant Swiss chard leaves
½ avocado
1 banana
1 cup strawberries
½ cup sunflower seeds
1 cup water
1 cup ice

Method

1. Blend the water, ice, and sunflower seeds for 30 seconds on very high speed.
2. Add the chard leaves and blend for another 10-20 seconds on high speed.
3. Add the banana, avocado, and strawberries and blend until thick and creamy.
4. Transfer to a cup or a portable jar and enjoy!

Tip: All berries are great sources of biotin, so use whatever berries you like on have on hand.

Nutritional Information (per serving)

Calories: 287
Fat Total: 16.4g
Carbohydrates: 33.8g
Protein: 6.9g
Dietary Fiber: 14.6g

Kale and Apple Detox Smoothie

Prep time: 5 minutes   Calories: 259   Serves: 2

This smoothie works best for an early morning after an over-indulging night. It will cleanse your system and give you a morning energy boost.

Ingredients

2 cups kale
2 Honey crisp apples
1 English cucumber
1 banana
2 tablespoons spirulina powder
1 cup water
1 cup ice

Method

1. Blend the spirulina with the water for at least 30 seconds on very high speed.
2. Add the ice and the veggies and blend for another 30 seconds.
3. Finally, add the apples and the banana and blend until well combined.
4. Transfer to a cup or a portable jar and enjoy!

Tip: You can also use maca powder or chlorella instead of the spirulina powder.

Nutritional Information (per serving)

Calories: 259
Fat Total: 0.8g
Carbohydrates: 61.6g
Protein: 8.5g
Dietary Fiber: 8.9g

Creamy Avocado Smoothie

Prep time: 5 minutes   Calories: 322   Serves: 2

Not only do avocados taste amazing, they are a true nutritional powerhouse. This creamy fruit is loaded with heart-healthy fats and antioxidants.

Ingredients

1 cup baby spinach
1 ripe avocado
1 cup strawberries
½ cup fresh orange juice
½ cup isotonic sports drink
1 tablespoon almond butter

Method

1. Blend the orange juice, sports drink, and almond butter for 30 seconds on high speed.
2. Add the spinach and the avocado and blend for another 10-20 seconds.
3. Add your fruits and blend until well combined.
4. Transfer to a cup or a portable jar and enjoy!

Tip: The almond butter provides some nutty crunch to balance the creaminess of the avocado, but by all means skip it if you prefer your smoothie to be as creamy as possible.

Nutritional Information (per serving)

Calories: 322
Fat Total: 24.6g
Carbohydrates: 24.8g
Protein: 13.7g
Dietary Fiber: 5.4g

Refreshing Cucumber Smoothie

Prep time: 5 minutes   Calories: 220   Serves: 2

Nothing beats this smoothie when it comes to cooling, yet healthy summer drinks. Not only does it provide great hydration in the summer heat, it is also loaded with minerals and electrolytes.

Ingredients

1 cup isotonic sport drink
2 English cucumbers
1 cup orange juice
4 tangerines
2 tablespoons fresh mint
1 cup ice

Method

1. Blend the sports drink, orange juice, fresh mint, and ice for 30 seconds on high speed.
2. Add the cucumbers and the tangerines and blend until well combined.
3. Transfer to a cup or a portable jar and enjoy!

Tip: This drink will have a texture closer to a juice made in a blender. You can even run it through a mesh sieve and it will turn into a silky smooth, refreshing summer beverage.

Nutritional Information (per serving)

Calories: 220
Fat Total: 1.2g
Carbohydrates: 52.7g
Protein: 5.2g
Dietary Fiber: 5.4g

Carrot Ginger Ale Smoothie

Prep time: 5 minutes   Calories: 169   Serves: 2

This smoothie is inspired by the classic ginger ale soft drink, but it comes with a carrot twist and a lot more health benefits.

Ingredients

1 cup orange juice
4 large carrots
2 tablespoons grated ginger
2 tablespoons lemon juice
1 tablespoon honey
1 cup ice

Method

1. Blend the orange juice, lemon juice, ice, and honey for 20 seconds on high speed.
2. Add the carrots and the ginger and blend on the highest possible setting until the carrots are all broken down and everything is well combined.
3. Transfer to a cup or a portable jar and enjoy!

Tip: You can add a splash of sparkling water right over your smoothie once you pour it into glasses or jars.

Nutritional Information (per serving)

Calories: 169
Fat Total: 1g
Carbohydrates: 39.5g
Protein: 2.8g
Dietary Fiber: 5.1g

Spinach Smoothie with Blueberry and Banana

Prep time: 5 minutes   Calories: 170   Serves: 2

This smoothie is dairy free, paleo friendly, and incredibly tasty. Add a scoop of vanilla protein powder and you can turn it into a great post-workout protein shake.

Ingredients

1 cup unsweetened almond milk
1 cup baby spinach
2 bananas
2 cups strawberries
a dash of cinnamon
1 cup ice

Method

1. Blend the almond milk, ice, and cinnamon for 30 seconds on high speed.
2. Add the spinach and blend for 10-20 seconds, or until the spinach is broken down.
3. Add the bananas and the strawberries and blend until well combined.
4. Transfer to a cup or a portable jar and enjoy!

Tip: If your bananas are not very ripe, you can add a tablespoon of honey to sweeten up your smoothie.

Nutritional Information (per serving)

Calories: 170
Fat Total: 1.7g
Carbohydrates: 39.1g
Protein: 3.1g
Dietary Fiber: 15.5g

Rainbow Chard and Blackberry Smoothie

Prep time: 5 minutes   Calories: 242   Serves: 2

This smoothie proves that even the bitterest greens will work as long as you combine them smartly.

Ingredients

1 cup water
2 bananas
4 giant rainbow chard leaves
1 cup blackberries
1 cup pineapple, cubed
1 tablespoon honey
a dash of cinnamon

Method

1. Blend the water with the honey and the cinnamon for 10 seconds on high speed, or until it gets frothy.
2. Add the chard and the blackberries and blend for 30 seconds on high speed.
3. Lastly, add the bananas and the pineapple and blend until well combined.
4. Transfer to a cup or a portable jar and enjoy!

Tip: Discard the stem of the chard leaves because it can have a bitter aftertaste.

Nutritional Information (per serving)

Calories: 242
Fat Total: 0.7g
Carbohydrates: 63.7g
Protein: 7.5g
Dietary Fiber: 11.8g

Green Monster Smoothie

Prep time: 5 minutes   Calories: 159   Serves: 2

Just as the name suggest, this smoothie comes with so much greens, nothing beats it for Monday morning detox after an over-indulging weekend.

Ingredients

1 cup water
1 cup kale
1 cup romaine lettuce
1 English cucumber
2 celery stalks
1 small bunch parsley
1 large banana
1 green apple

Method

1. Blend the water with the kale and the romaine lettuce for 30 seconds on high speed.
2. Add the remaining veggies and blend for another 10-20 seconds on high speed.
3. Add the banana and the apple and blend until well combined.
4. Transfer to a cup or a portable jar and enjoy!

Tip: Don't add more fruit to sweeten the smoothie. If the green taste is too much for you to handle, add a tablespoon of honey or agave nectar.

Nutritional Information (per serving)

Calories: 159
Fat Total: 0.6g
Carbohydrates: 43.1g
Protein: 3.9g
Dietary Fiber: 7.7g

Summer Herbs Smoothie

Prep time: 5 minutes   Calories: 236   Serves: 2

This smoothie is so simple to put together, but it comes exploding with summer herbs flavors and aromas. You'll never want to sip on a boring lemonade ever again.

Ingredients

2 cups fresh orange juice
1 cup water
2 tangerines
1 cup baby spinach
4 tablespoons fresh mint
2 tablespoons fresh basil
1 cup ice

Method

1. Blend the orange juice and the ice for 30 seconds on high speed.
2. Add the tangerines and blend for another 10 to 20 seconds on high speed.
3. Add the spinach and the herbs and blend until well combined.
4. Transfer to a cup or a portable jar and enjoy!

Tip: You can also add a tablespoon of fresh rosemary.

Nutritional Information (per serving)

Calories: 236
Fat Total: 1g
Carbohydrates: 55.6g
Protein: 5g
Dietary Fiber: 4.7g

Kale Wellness Smoothie

Prep time: 5 minutes   Calories: 435   Serves: 2

This wellness smoothie is filled with green veggies, antioxidant-rich berries, and heart-healthy seeds to help you drink your way into health.

Ingredients

2 cups kale
2 celery stalks
1 cup iceberg
½ cup cranberries
½ cup blueberries
1 banana
1 tablespoon chlorella
2 tablespoons flax seeds
2 tablespoons chia seeds
1 cup coconut water

Method

1. Blend the coconut water with the chlorella, flax, and chia seeds for 30 seconds on high speed.
2. Add the veggies and the banana and blend for another 10-20 seconds on high speed.
3. In the end, add the berries and blend until well combined.
4. Transfer to a cup or a portable jar and enjoy!

Tip: You can soak the chia seeds in the coconut water until they turn gelatinous. This will give your smoothie a thicker texture.

Nutritional Information (per serving)

Calories: 435
Fat Total: 13.9g
Carbohydrates: 62.3g
Protein: 16.1g
Dietary Fiber: 21g

Tropical Pea Smoothie

Prep time: 5 minutes   Calories: 198   Serves: 2

No one says you should only stick to leafy greens for your smoothies; in fact, frozen peas are an amazing nutritious addition to smoothies. They are naturally sweet and filled with fiber, iron, and Vitamin C.

Ingredients

1 cup water
½ cup frozen peas
2 cups strawberries
1 cup pineapple cubes
2 tangerines
a dash of cinnamon

Method

1. Blend the water with the peas, strawberries, and cinnamon for 30 seconds on high speed.
2. Add the pineapple and the tangerines and blend until well combined.
3. Transfer to a cup or a portable jar and enjoy!

Tip: Add a cup of ice if you're using fresh peas.

Nutritional Information (per serving)

Calories: 198
Fat Total: 0.8g
Carbohydrates: 51.2g
Protein: 5.7g
Dietary Fiber: 16.5g

Broccoli Smoothie with Raspberry and Yogurt

Prep time: 5 minutes   Calories: 198   Serves: 2

Broccoli is another amazing green vegetable to add to your smoothies: not only is it known as one of the healthiest foods, it also has a very neutral taste, so you'll never know that you're sipping on broccoli with your morning drink.

Ingredients

1 cup nonfat Greek yogurt
1 cup broccoli florets
1 banana
2 cups raspberries
½ cup water
a dash of cinnamon
1 cup ice

Method

1. Blend the water, Greek yogurt, ice, and cinnamon for 30 seconds on high speed.
2. Add the broccoli florets and blend for another 10-20 seconds.
3. Lastly, add the banana and raspberries and blend until well combined.
4. Transfer to a cup or a portable jar and enjoy!

Tip: Any berries you might already have on hand will work with this smoothie.

Nutritional Information (per serving)

Calories: 198
Fat Total: 1.1g
Carbohydrates: 37.8g
Protein: 15.2g
Dietary Fiber: 11.6g

Virgin Bloody Mary Smoothie

Prep time: 5 minutes   Calories: 195   Serves: 1

This smoothie is inspired by the classic Bloody Mary cocktail, but it comes in a healthy, morning smoothie version that will fill you up fiber and antioxidants.

Ingredients

1 cup tomato juice
1 cup cherry tomatoes
2 celery stalks
1 bunch cilantro
½ cup apple juice
2 tablespoons lime juice
a few drops hot sauce

Method

1. Blend the tomato juice, apple juice, lime juice, and hot sauce for 30 seconds on high speed.
2. Add the cilantro, celery, and tomatoes and blend until well combined.
3. Transfer to a cup or a portable jar and enjoy!

Tip: Sneak in a splash of vodka for those long, relaxing weekend mornings.

Nutritional Information

Calories: 195
Fat Total: 1.6g
Carbohydrates: 45.6g
Protein: 7.7g
Dietary Fiber: 8.8g

Cucumber Lime Smoothie

Prep time: 5 minutes   Calories: 324   Serves: 1

This smoothie tastes like a lime sorbet: sweet, tart, and incredibly cooling on a hot summer morning.

Ingredients

1 English cucumber
4 tablespoons lime juice
1 frozen banana
½ cup nonfat Greek yogurt
1 tablespoon honey
1 cup ice

Method

1. Blend the yogurt, lime juice, and honey for 30 seconds on high speed.
2. Add the cucumber and the banana and blend for another 10-20 seconds on high speed.
3. Add the ice in the end and blend until it gets to a sorbet consistency.
4. Transfer to a cup or a portable jar and enjoy!

Tip: Add more ice if you're using a fresh banana.

Nutritional Information

Calories: 324
Fat Total: 0.7g
Carbohydrates: 74.5g
Protein: 15.2g
Dietary Fiber: 6.1g

Tropical Carrot Smoothie

Prep time: 5 minutes   Calories: 195   Serves: 2

This smoothie has an amazing orange color and is filled with beta-carotenes, Vitamin C, and fiber to kick-start your metabolism in the morning.

Ingredients

1 ripe mango
½ cup fresh orange juice
½ cup carrot juice
3 medium carrots
2 tangerines
a dash of cinnamon
1 cup ice

Method

1. Blend the orange juice, carrot juice, ice, and cinnamon for 30 seconds on high speed.
2. Add the carrots and blend for another 10-20 seconds.
3. Cut the mango into large chunks and add it to your blender along with the tangerines. Blend until well combined.
4. Transfer to a cup or a portable jar and enjoy!

Tip: Pineapple will also work with this smoothie, but it will bring some tartness to the drink, making it less sweet.

Nutritional Information (per serving)

Calories: 195
Fat Total: 0.7g
Carbohydrates: 47.4g
Protein: 2.8g
Dietary Fiber: 6.2g

Spinach Antioxidant Smoothie

Prep time: 5 minutes   Calories: 227   Serves: 2

Spinach is very easy for digestion, pomegranate helps provide relief from stress, and the berries are just bursting with antioxidants, making this smoothie a perfectly rounded morning meal.

Ingredients

1 cup pomegranate juice
1 cup baby spinach
1 cup strawberries
1 cup blueberries
1 cup blackberries
1 frozen banana

Method

1. Blend the pomegranate juice with the spinach for 30 seconds on high speed.
2. Add the berries and blend for another 10-20 seconds.
3. In the end add the banana and blend until well combined.
4. Transfer to a cup or a portable jar and enjoy!

Tip: Raspberries or cranberries will also work well with this smoothie.

Nutritional Information (per serving)

Calories: 227
Fat Total: 0.9g
Carbohydrates: 55.4g
Protein: 3g
Dietary Fiber: 13.2g

Sweet Romaine Smoothie

Prep time: 5 minutes   Calories: 250   Serves: 2

Crisp romaine lettuce is a very nutritious veggie, packing tons of protein, iron, calcium, and Vitamin A in a single serving.

Ingredients

2 cups romaine lettuce
1 cup isotonic sports drink
½ cup fresh orange juice
1 apple
1 English cucumber
1 banana
1 small mango
4 tablespoons sunflower seeds
1 cup ice

Method

1. Blend the sports drink with the orange juice and the ice for 30 seconds on high speed.
2. Add the lettuce, cucumber, and sunflower seeds and blend for another 10-20 seconds.
3. Add all your fruits and blend until well combined.
4. Transfer to a cup or a portable jar and enjoy!

Tip: You can mix up the fruits by substituting a pear for the apple, and some berries for the mango. You can also use pumpkin seeds instead of the sunflower seeds.

Nutritional Information (per serving)

Calories: 250
Fat Total: 3.8g
Carbohydrates: 53.7g
Protein: 4.7g
Dietary Fiber: 8.3g

Conclusion

Thank you again for purchasing this book!

I hope you enjoyed the recipes and get many years of use out of them in my book on **Weight Loss On the Go with Tasty Detox Smoothie Recipes.**

Finally, if you enjoyed this book, please take the time to share your thoughts and write me an honest review about the book – I truly value your opinion and thoughts and I will incorporate them into my next book, which is already underway. **Please post your review on Amazon.** (just type the title - **Weight Loss On the Go with Tasty Detox Smoothie Recipes** – in the Amazon URL and the page will come up to enter reviews). It'd be GREATLY appreciated. A kind review is always helpful and keeps me inspired.

Thank you and to Great, Healthy Eating.

Maria Bertoli

Hello,

Maybe like you, I enjoy finding new recipes and creating my own recipes, especially when I can keep the prep time less than 15 or 20 minutes, unless it's a special meal I'm making.

However, I love spending time with my family a whole lot more, especially that special little fellow I'm holding in the picture. That's our grandson, Alex. He's our center of pride and joy, along with his father (our son), and his wife.

My husband (of 36+ years) and I are putting together our favorite recipes which take the minimum amount of prep time, but yield a delicious meal!!

We hope you enjoy each of our books in the Food Recipe Series. We'll be including everything from a Healthy 2 Week Meal Plan to the Ultimate Mouthwatering Pizzas and much, much more.

All our books and recipes can be found at www.YourCenterforRecipes.com. This will be a continually growing site as we add our recipes for all kinds of foods and our reader's special recipes that they would like to share. Please come and join us and think about sending in your favorite recipe. Who knows, you might find your recipe and name in one of our upcoming books!!

Feel free to contact me at Maria@YourCenterforRecipes.com.

Till then, take care and enjoy that healthy eating (as well as a little splurge once in a while – we all need that!!).

Maria Bertoli

Please, Check out Our Other Books at Their Amazon URLs

A 2 Week Healthy, Easy Meal Plan

http://www.amazon.com/dp/B00JBNWYYC

10 Mouthwatering DIY Pizza Recipes

http://www.amazon.com/dp/B00K2279ZU

Healthy, Refreshing Salad Recipes for Anytime

http://www.amazon.com/dp/B00K0R7Q1O